# Come Into My Place

# Come Into My Place

## A Collection of Love Poems

## Melissa Emily Mitchell

authorHOUSE®

AuthorHouse™
1663 Liberty Drive
Bloomington, IN 47403
www.authorhouse.com
Phone: 1-800-839-8640

First published by AuthorHouse   05/20/2011

ISBN: 978-1-4634-0748-3 (sc)
ISBN: 978-1-4634-0747-6 (ebk)

Library of Congress Control Number:  2011907281

Printed in the United States of America

Photography by: Peter Hurley Photography, a division of Hurley Productions LLC

Any people depicted in stock imagery provided by Thinkstock are models, and such images are being used for illustrative purposes only.
Certain stock imagery © Thinkstock.

This book is printed on acid-free paper.

# Contents

V. <u>Inspirations</u> ........................................71

# _Foreword_

_Come Into My Place_ is an invitation. Those who have chosen to accept will receive verses of love, reflections of life, and inspiration to find what is precious in their own lives and worth sharing with others.

Poetry, in my eyes, constitutes so many amazing and intriguing things. It allows me to capture my life's moments fearlessly. There are no inhibitions with Poetry.

My passion for love and this journey in life has inspired these written expressions you will read . . . they are all pieces of me. I gather them up and pour them out to you . . . it is a place all your own . . . Enjoy!

Melissa Emily Mitchell
April 20, 2011


"Once, tears were the fire extinguisher
to the love flames that burned in me . . ."

# _Dedication_

_This book is dedicated to my mother, Marilyn P. Parrott and my father, the late Ralph T. Mitchell, Sr. who filled me with an abundance of love and support from the beginning. If it weren't for this overflow of love, I may not have been able to communicate my most intimate thoughts and invite my readers into my heart. You are my foundation. I am forever grateful and so in love with you both._

# Just M.E.

# The Black Poet

Curly kinky hair
Golden brown skin
Full lips, long eyelashes
Bold and beautiful
Curvaceous frame
She writes
In the dark, that is
She writes of her life
The good, the bad, the ugly
Of the experiences, the daily encounters
Of the people who enrich her life
She is a retrospective poet
She flips each element of the past
To fit who she is right now
Day by day, she sees herself growing
Behind closed doors
She is a refugee
A wall is built between her and the outside world
And where she finds peace and tranquility
An escape route from evil and all sorts of
negativity
Positive feeds off positive energy
Surrounding herself with positive people brings
positivity
Positive she is trying to be
And stay

*A black poet in the prime of her life*
*Recognizing who she is and who she has become*
*No more black poet hiding in the dark*
*Black poet will appear in the light*

# **The Color Purple**

*I am in the purple room*
*And I'm feeling quite royal*
*Decked out in the finest jewels*
*Surrounded by my golden throne*
*I am screaming royalty*
*All over*
*My crown is rolling stones*
*Purple stones*
*And my smile is glowing*
*Warm, sweet, free-spirited*
*I am a*
*Queen*

*Melissa Emily Mitchell*

# On A Late Night Stroll

*Raindrops falling*
*Midnight approaching*
*As I step out into the rain*
*I am soaking wet with stories to tell*
*My footsteps lightly walk the pavement*
*I have one thousand and one ideas flowing*
*inside of me*
*I see traffic lights*
*I see boys on the corner*
*Not men*
*Getting their hustle bustle on*
*As I walk through the streets tonight I pay close*
*attention*
*Instead of picking up the pace*
*I slow down to admire my surroundings*
*You know what they say*
*Home Sweet Home*
*To me it is more like*
*Home Home Home*
*Tick Tock Tick Tock*
*The clock is watching*
*And so are the people*
*They say a young lady never walks the streets*
*late at night*
*At least not when dark approaches*
*It is called un-lady like*

*But you know what I have to say right?*
*Never judge a book by its cover*
*If you were all up in my business*
*You would know that I am a poet in motion*
*A poet on yet another excursion*
*To artistically and poetically capture*
*All my surroundings in the palm of my hands*
*Letting each moment of my experiences*
*Fall down around my soft fingertips and onto*
*pieces of white paper*
*I am very much a young lady, I say*
*Maybe you should try finding you one!*

Melissa Emily Mitchell

# I am Growing

I find that my current state of mind
Is too complex for most individuals
Tainted by the shortcomings
Haphazards and temporary pleasures of life
Most individuals' thoughts speak very limited
Simple-minded ways
Simple-minded actions
I find that the focus for most is on today
What will I get out of today?
Instead of: What can I give someone today?
I am a spectator of growth between human
beings
I am realizing my own progressions
And realizing the lack thereof in others
Growth is a beautiful thing
It is amazing to look back on
And inspiring to see what lies ahead
If you continue to move forward
Like an audio cassette tape of your favorite song
It is nothing like that very first time
The first time you hear it
The rhythm of the music
Is like sweet melodies to your ear
As you continue to play it
A third and fourth time

*Rewind. Replay. Rewind. Replay.*
*The rhythm doesn't quite sound the same*
*Never like the first time*
*You must know that this idea of growing out of*
*old things*
*And growing accustomed to new things speaks*
*of*
*Life, love, and many situations and experiences*
*Subliminally*

*Melissa Emily Mitchell*

# My Poetry Is My High

*My poetry is my high*
*Sometimes I crave it*
*Other times, I feel like I'm going through*
*withdrawal*
*Sometimes I'm filled with so many emotions*
*Sometimes I have little emotion at all*
*It all depends on what I'm going through*
*And the ending of a situation I see myself coming*
*to*
*My poetry is my high*
*Sometimes I crave it*
*Other times, I reject it*
*I feel like I'm going through withdrawal*

# To Those Not Yet Tainted

*Keep away*
*You need to protect you*
*From a confused little girl*
*Who wouldn't know a good thing*
*If it slapped her right in the face*
*Fell on her lap*
*And God handed it to her generously*
*You are not supposed to be here*
*You are not supposed to love so free and*
*unconditionally*
*In this world your love should be conditioned - - -*
*Hell! It should be conditioned, shampooed,*
*flip-flopped,*
*Sick, twisted, tainted all kinds of ways*
*Have you not been hit with reality?*
*Were you born yesterday?*
*Why do you keep giving your love away?*
*The confused wants to know*
*He whispered: "Today, I am man of God*
*Tomorrow, I remain the same*
*I live for the Lord*
*Not for the masses*
*If I didn't*
*I'd be a dead man walking and driven myself*
*insane"*

# A Father's Love

## Dedicated to My Father

*The love between a father and his daughter*
*Supersedes the love shared between a man and*
*his woman*
*A father treats his daughter like the woman he*
*loves*
*With respect, honesty, love, and appreciation*
*He shows her how a young woman*
*A woman of God*
*A woman filled with love*
*Should be treated*
*The love between a father and his daughter*
*should be cherished*
*A father cannot teach his daughter how to be a*
*woman*
*However, he can instill certain morals and values*
*in her*
*To help her define her understanding of life, love,*
*and happiness*
*All the while ensuring her recognition of her own*
*self worth*
*The love between a father and his daughter*
*Supersedes the love shared between a man and*
*his woman*
*The love between a man and his woman*
*Is fashioned*

*It takes time and effort to build and work to
sustain
The love between a father and his daughter
Is infused from the moment his baby girl is
conceived
The love remains pure—
Never selfish or boastful or inhibited
It's continuous*

# A Dedication to Mother

*I am proud to be a product of you*
*I love to represent who you are*
*You are a beautiful person*
*Mother*
*And with each step of my heart*
*I say I love you*
*With long black hair*
*And a coca-cola shaped figure*
*Fairly proportioned at the top*
*Bottle pop at the bottom*
*Having all the fellas gazing*
*Product of she is me*
*Same almond shaped eyes*
*Soft skin*
*Comfortable in the skin I am in*
*Why*
*Because I am a reflection of my mother*

# And Then . . . There Was This Thing Called Love

# To Have,
# To Hold Love

*To have and to hold love*
*To hug and to kiss love*
*To squeeze and caress love*
*Oh, how it feels to love*
*To be in love*
*To share with one love*
*To grasp the hands of love*
*Oh, how it feels to touch love*
*To feed thy soul with love*
*To live and breathe with love*
*To smell the sweet scent of love*
*Oh, how it feels to taste love*
*To become one with love*
*To see that to breathe*
*And to feel*
*And to touch*
*And to taste love*
*Is love*
*Love is surely what thou makest*

# Serenity

*I am as liberated and free as I want to be*
*I am as smooth as the waves that flow against*
*the sea*
*I am as calm and peaceful as the ocean*
*Me and my Romeo are paddling our lives away*
*Along the river*
*With no destination at all*
*Just me and him*
*Him and I*
*On our way to a life of eternal bliss*

# The Way You Make Me Feel

*The beats of my heart*
*Are as loud as the African drums that speak*
*When you come around*
*My mouth becomes moist*
*As I inhale and exhale your sweet scent*
*Imagining how delicious you taste*
*My palms become sweaty*
*As I imagine you loving me*
*Slowly touching and teasing me*
*Caressing and pleasing me*
*My knees become weak*
*As you ask me to be your eternal Nubian queen*
*To have and to hold till death we part*
*As I accept my entire body is at freeze*
*A stand still, my body is frozen*
*From my hair follicles to my ten toes on my two*
*feet*
*But it is not cold feet, I say*
*My body is burning hot*
*Hot because you got me on fire*
*360° degrees inside a cold, cold world*

# A Love Anthem

Let me stroke you like the morning breeze
On a warm summer day
Underneath the tree
Let that be our hideaway
We can talk about the moon
We can talk about the stars
We can talk about our past
And how we've become who we are
I wanna rock your mind
And make love to your soul all night long
I wanna cuddle with your intellect
And I'll return the warmth with my intelligence
Let's explode with honesty and integrity
And end the love session with sincerity
I wanna rock your mind
And make love to your soul all night long
I wanna caress your sensitiveness
And as I listen to your story
Let you know you are not alone
Let's have a mental love session
You bring the knowledge and I'll bring the truth
Together we can slowly make melodies of true
love

# O-h My

When I think of you and me
I think not of how fly this young guy is
Or
Even more
How cute it would look if you and I
Were to walk through the streets of Harlem
tonight
I think not of the reasons why you caught my
eyes
That first time
When I noticed you noticing me
Noticing you
You were standing not far from me
Arms distance, I believe
When I had the sudden desire to act upon
feelings
Of spontaneous erotic intimacy
I imagined you loving me
No! It was more like . . .
I felt the sweet sensation of your love
Before it was even given to me freely
I knew I wanted to sneak up on your love
Take it
Before you could even see
Or think twice about handing it over
At the same time

*I questioned whether I could handle you
handling me
If I let you
And that this idea of you and me
If I put you and I together at that time
Could very well be just a sexual attraction
Minus the intellectual stability I knew we would
need
If we planned to get to know each other better
Confident as you and I wanted to be
We eventually initiated conversation
Which led to more conversation
Which led to friendship with
How shall I say
Minor adjustments and benefits
Maybe one day it will lead to . . .*

# Declined In Response to Nikki Giovanni's "I Take MasterCard (Charge Your Love to Me)"

*Your credit is bad*
*You're no longer pre-approved*
*As a matter of fact*
*You might as well declare bankruptcy*
*You're so overdrawn*
*Your limit is overdue*
*My time is up*
*And those stories about you not deserving me*
*Have surfaced once again*
*Your services have been rendered*
*You're no longer being used*
*MasterCard is no good*
*Visa is out the door*
*American Express and Discover*
*My love don't live there no more*
*Interest has accrued*
*So pay up*

*Troubled women don't know where your secrets
lie yet
I'm sure you'll find one that will fall for the
foolishness
But not me
I am troubled no more
No more credit
Bad credit that is
I take my payments up front
Charge it to the game*

# **Fulfillment**

*The smell of vanilla coffee beans*
*Roasting on the fire*
*The fire in my eyes*
*Which if you look close enough*
*Will tell you how hot you make me feel*
*The feeling I get inside*
*As I bring the tea of herbs to the table*
*And light the scented candle*
*Candle of love is lit*
*Light me up with all the love you have to give*
*Spread me out*
*Like the butter on the warm rolls inside the oven*
*Dinner is on me*
*Literally*
*You see by the time you get through loving me*
*Me is I*
*I am now the feast*
*More like you've had the entrées and the*
*appetizers*
*But I am enough to fill you*
*I am the full course meal*
*Bow your head and say your grace*
*Bless the Lord for allowing you to receive me*
*And slowly dig in*
*Making sure you digest every bit*
*Carefully*

*Melissa Emily Mitchell*

# Just a Touch Away

*In the middle of the night*
*I lay here wanting to be next to you*
*As I rest my head on my pillow*
*Illusions upon illusions*
*I imagine your silhouette*
*Walking barefoot on the bare floor*
*Baring nothing but skin*
*Right now*
*Right this very moment*
*I want to jump your bones*
*There are three types of love*
*Romantic love, friendly love, and consummate*
*love*
*Baby you consume me*
*Do you understand what that means?*
*You are my supreme*
*Together we are one*
*You are my alpha and omega*
*When you make love to me*
*Love so sweet, so tender*
*You keep me on a high*

*A natural high*
*Let's complete this feeling*
*Let's come together as one*
*When I am with you*
*I am never alone*
*When you are far*
*You are never too far*
*Because I keep you in my heart, in my mind, in*
*my soul*
*Tonight when I open my eyes*
*My hopes are that you and I*
*Will be here alone tonight*
*You by my side where you belong*

*Melissa Emily Mitchell*

# That Night

*That night I wore white garment*
*Silk was its trim*
*You undressed me and laid me down*
*In a bed of white roses*
*We had a sip of white wine*
*And as you gently caressed my face*
*Then my body, then my lips*
*You pressed against your own*
*And we began to make love*
*Pure, passionate love*
*Clear juices flowed*
*As our bodies became one on the white satin*
*pillows*
*Where we rest our heads as we rest our souls*
*In the morning, as the sun rose*
*We lay in each others arms*
*Confident and comfortable with this union*
*You and I*
*And in the garden of love*
*We harvest a babe*

# By the Waterfront

*Imagine me*
*Loving you*
*By the Waterfront*
*As the waves go in and out*
*We passionately make love*
*In and out, in and out*
*Time has ceased as far as my clock is concerned*
*All that matters is right now*
*This very moment*
*I am not thinking about the events in the past*
*Or the aftermath of this intimate lovemaking*
*Like Vivian Green sang*
*You-got-me-on-an-emotional-roller-coaster*
*I knew your love was toxic*
*It was never good for me*
*But*
*What the hell*
*I am trying to get my groove on like Stella*
*Even if it is only temporary*

# **Shipwrecked**

*I stayed praying you would change*
*But you didn't*
*I avoided confrontation with my heart*
*I couldn't let it know*
*That deep down inside there was no hope for*
*you*
*And I was slowly drowning in my own self worth*
*I was hopelessly in love*
*So I thought*
*How dangerous loving you had become*
*For my mind, body, and soul were no more*
*I had lost all my dignity*
*And like a ship lost at sea*
*I was gone, so far gone*
*If I had tried to come back and be rescued*
*I couldn't*

# Just a New York State of Mind

Caught up in the struggle
So used to the New York City streets
Gangsta life, gangsta thug
Nowhere to go, no one to trust
Like a black girl lost
Black man lost
No equality in the equal opportunity system
Not for the typical black man in America
One who grew up way too fast
With enough on his plate
Only to later add a criminal background
To this previously existing anti-black man world
Got wifey at home with a college degree in her
hand
About to go for her master's degree
Her only wish for him is that he better himself
The best way he can
And be all that he can be
Whether it be
To live out his passionate dream in the music
business
Or going back to school
Whatever her baby boy desires
She is there for her king
Through and through
All his ups and downs

31

Baby girl is doing well
But baby boy is struggling
Trying to compete with the world outside
Just for his eternal nubian queen
Things are getting harder
He can't keep up
The world has got on its running shoes
Sprinting 3.25 seconds
And he is
Left behind
Where is wifey
Nubian queen, baby girl
She is still by his side
But the story ends like this
She pushed and pushed him
As much as she could
Until she began to see herself slowing down
It wasn't until a little while ago
She had to leave him completely alone
And get herself back on track
And not end up like him
Black. Lost.

# **Perplexed**

*How do I reach someone who doesn't quite
understand me?*
*If I sat down and read him or her the story of my
life*
*Could I expect him or her to comprehend?*
*To accept me as I am with all my complexities
and*
*Uncertainties*
*Am I just a lost soul in a world all by myself?*
*Or is it that I have become to serious with my life*
*And I am so far gone?*
*Is it possible to develop a relationship*
*Any relationship*
*If the two cannot relate to each other at all?*

*Melissa Emily Mitchell*

# **Till Kingdom Come**

*Like a woman gone blind*
*You had me shut-eyed to the lies*
*And I'll tell you today*
*How his story became my story*
*The story of you and I*
*One of pain and passion*
*Glitter and glitz*
*From a fairytale story*
*To one of distress and distraught*
*Like a queen in a kingdom enthrone*
*I was enthroned*
*Then dethroned*
*But not without finding out*
*My king found a new queen to take my place*
*Could she ever really be me?*
*What I was to you when I was*
*What I was to you when I wasn't*
*Royalty could not be she*
*Loyalty is not he*
*Kingdom*
*Yes, that's right*
*King is dumb for leaving this queen*
*Queen of royalty and loyalty*
*He tries to put her to shame*
*But only he looks foolish*

# **Untitled**

When I see joy

           *I see pain*

When I see laughter

          *I see sadness*

When I see hope

          *I see despair*

When I see you

          *I see me*

We

      *Could never be*

*Melissa Emily Mitchell*

# Coin Toss

With a gentle toss
It flipped up
It flipped down
Slick, slippery, and silver
If one took a closer look at my hand
The sweat on my inner palm
Could tell you just how bad the odds were
Heads up
I saw the head
But before I could move
The tail knocked me out

# **Foolishplay**

*I became this actress in this screenplay called*
*Love*
*Since then I've lost my sight, my ability to listen,*
*reason*
*And act beyond my senses*
*I once had a face*
*But I don't have one anymore*
*If I do, then it's somebody else's*
*I can no longer recognize who I used to be*
*I am caught up in the realm of Love*
*Who have I become*
*And what happened to the real me?*

Melissa Emily Mitchell

# My Love Triad

*I am in a place all by myself*
*Facing fears*
*Jumping obstacles*
*I cry because it's the only way to release*
*My anxiety*
*My frustration*
*My rage*

*I'm sad*
*I thought I was ready to give the man I say I love*
*The Key*
*So he could*
*Graciously un-lock Love who lies inside of me*
*A rude awakening—*

*I'm mad*
*I am exposed to the wicked world of baby-mama*
*drama*
*Bloody, gruesome quarrels*
*Sleeping on sofas or living room floors*
*Instead of in my bed with me*
*He says "why should you get mad, I come home*
*to you every night"?*
*Is that justification for your ass?*

*Hell No!*
*The man is not really a man*

*If he cannot grasp hold of the situation at hand*
*Stop lolly-gagging and*
*Acting like a sissy pants!*
*You see, I love my man*
*I don't mean to come down on him*

*But when the snake*
*I mean the young stupid girl who opened her legs*
*Whose egg met sperm and created life*
*Slithers her way inside this realm of happiness*
*and tranquility*
*She spits venom*
*She is vindictive*
*She evokes anger and frustration in me with her*
*juvenile stupidity*

*She poisons the minds of children—even her own*
*No one—I mean no one will triumph over me*
*I am me*
*That lioness*
*Confident in stride*
*A bit boastful, head held high*
*Queen of the Jungle*
*Passionate about my lover, my protector, my*
*friend,*
*My man, who possess hands that don't stroke*
*you or hold you like they used to*

*Youngster, come on you had your chance*
*Who Am I?*
*I am*
*The better woman now in demand*
*And no one can be the victor but me*

*Melissa Emily Mitchell*

# The Nerve of You

*The nerve of you*
*To take control and steal my heart away*
*The nerve of you*
*To listen in on my fears and work against those*
*night and day*
*The nerve of you*
*To sneak up on me when I'm most vulnerable*
*To enter my life and turn it upside down*
*How dare you come along*
*Take back all your shit*
*All the lies and alibis*
*Give me my sanity back*
*You're so far out there*
*I never want to see you again*
*Go back to the circus you silly sly bear*
*"I hate you so much right now"*
*I don't think you heard me*
*"I hate you so much right now"*
*Give me back my time*
*Give me back my laughter and sunshine*
*Oh, you just don't understand*
*Right now, I wish I had a 9!*

# Stanza 3

*The last time I loved you was the last time I lived
in*
                                              *Vain*

*When we were together I cursed you each and*
                                        *Every time*

*The day we met was the saddest day of my*

                    *Life*

*Melissa Emily Mitchell*

# Foolish Man's Pride

*If it was just you and I alone in a room*
*I would undress the majestic overcoat you hold*
*so tightly around you called Pride*
*I would uncover all the ideas and reasons behind*
*Why you played Russian roulette with my heart*
*You stole my love and gambled with my emotions*
*The razzle-dazzle display of affection*
*Could not fool me*
*I knew something was wrong*
*I am a recovering addict*
*Two years clean and going strong*
*Recovering from being addicted and strung out*
*on your love*
*Don't worry about me now*
*I'm doing just fine*
*Years later*
*Alone in a room*
*I pity you*
*I want to undress the pride inside your lonely*
*displeasured heart*
*And ask you to finally be a man of your*
*convictions*
*Or is it too late for you to start*
*Deep down inside*
*I want to ask*
*Why?*

*But a more important question is*
*Where are you now?*
*Have you learned what it means to be a man of*
*your word?*

# A Strange Encounter

I wanted to call you
Tossing and turning
My body wanted to hold you
In the late night hour
I could feel you caress me
Then slowly undress me
We made love like the very first time
Where you explored my insides
Touching each and every part of me like a cold
wind
I swear I could see and feel the butterflies within
Chills up and down my spine
No one could have said that you weren't mine
Because the way we made love, sweet love
Was like a blessing only the one above could
create
We were one
Soul mates
So who would have known
You left me abandoned
All alone
Now twenty years later, I am sitting in the same
chair
Where
We loved
Recollecting the events of the past

*Reviewing the elements of the last fifteen*
*seconds of my life*
*A quick encounter it was*
*But it hit me like the instant resistance of a drug/*
*addict/recovered*
*I jerked back on the corner of Seventh Street and*
*Ninth*
*You bumped into me as I bumped into you*
*We kept on going but the truth was in between*
*us*
*We were not strangers*
*We were lovers once*
*We were each other once*
*And it was those eyes I recognized again*
*Tonight*

# New Beginnings

# No Man's Land

*Captivate my soul*

*Take me away to*

*No Man's Land*

*I need to live in peace*

*At last!*

*Melissa Emily Mitchell*

# Roles of Life

*Everyone has a part to play*
*Which part will it be today?*
*The loving wife who stays at home*
*Passing her life away*
*Will it be the working woman*
*Or the feminist who tiptoes her way through life*
*Not giving a shit damn*
*About a man who offers her the world*
*She's just out to get her feminist stripe*
*Will you be the young woman*
*Who sets out to get her degree*
*With a collection of plaques on the wall*
*But dry as the drought on the driest desert day*
*Because she gets no lovin' at all*
*Too busy getting her education*
*To stop and release her frustrations*
*Everyone has a part to play*
*Which part will you play today?*

# Melodies of My Life

*I was born music*
*It is as if my surrogate mother is hip-hop*
*Oh, how hip-hop rocks*
*And there is no one cuter*
*Than my brother R&B*
*As my life changes*
*So does what I speak for and listen to*
*I am a representation of sweet melodies*
*Notes—some high and some low*

*Melissa Emily Mitchell*

# Catch Me If You Can

*Catch me if you can*
*I'll be in the leaves*
*As you pick up the pace*
*I'll leap forward*
*Hastily, keeping the rhythm of the music*
*As you reach for me, I'll roar*
*Showing my strong, fearless entity*
*I'll protect my surroundings*
*As I lie in the grass*
*Prowling my prey*
*I'll clean my paws*
*I'll regroup*
*The firmness of my stance*
*The redness of my eyes*
*The quest begins once again*
*Catch me if you can*

# Pieces

## Of


# M.E . . . .

# **Hoodwinked**

*Hey pretender*

*I thought I knew you so well*

*But, I guess I didn't*

# A Burlesque Poem

*I slept with a fairytale last night*

*And woke up with a busted pumpkin and no prince*

*This morning*

# A Found Poem from "My Love Triad"

*In between your court cases and baby mama
drama and your job that works you overtime
Where do I fit in?
On the next bus, getting to the next stop called
dodge!*

*Melissa Emily Mitchell*

# A Concrete Poem

*You say you love me*          *You say you don't want me to leave*

*Peace*

*But then you don't call*          *So I'm saying*

# Free Verse (vs.) M.E.

*When a man or woman doesn't inspire you,*
*When a man or woman doesn't admire you,*
*When a man or woman doesn't pay you*
*a compliment or two,*
*When a man or woman is lifeless,*
*It's time to move on*

*Melissa Emily Mitchell*

# An Epigram

*You are a backwards ass*

*You read everything the wrong way*

*So read this*

*! GOD EYBDOOG*

# **Flirt**

*Just because you're fine*
*Don't mean you can get it*
*Hmmm . . . what?*
*Wink*

*Melissa Emily Mitchell*

# Just Another Burlesque Poem

*I thought about you*
*Then I thought about us*
*Then I thought . . .*
*Why haven't I heard from you?*
*And then I stopped thinking!*

# **Lyrics**

*After thought*
*After the thought*
*Of leaving you*
*I couldn't*

*Melissa Emily Mitchell*

# Breathe
# (Just Another Free Verse Poem)

*Like Jasmine incense*
*I inhale and exhale you*
*And then deal with this dry ass reality of you*
*and me*
*And let you burn*

# **Wonderin'**

*I was just wonderin'*
*If you plan on stickin' around*
*You don't even have to mention love*
*Just keep makin' me smile*

*Melissa Emily Mitchell*

# Instant Replay

*In my mind*
*I see an instant replay of my past*
*Happening now*
*And press "Pause"!*

# Look Alike

*They said we looked good together*
*But*
*They didn't know you had a twin*

# Getting the Run Around

*So what's it gonna be?*
*Run around the words*
*And see if I can catch?*
*Game Over!*

# Untitled #2

*People say I'm nice*
*There are a few who say I'm bourgeois*
*What the hell*
*I'm both!*

# Inspirations

# What Inspires You? My Favorite Love Quotes

*"If you are born a woman you must never lend anymore than what you can afford to lose. This includes your heart."* ~Asha Bandele

*"His lifetime has expired."* ~Nina Elcock

*"God bless the child that has her own."* ~ Nana

*"Don't preoccupy myself with unfulfilling relationships."* ~Unknown

*"Embrace Inner Authority, Create Loving Experiences, Run Toward Life."* ~ Sherri Argov

*"Do not compromise for the sake of having a man (or woman)!"* ~ Sherri Argov

*"Many men will come, many men will try, you don't owe them nothing move slow and wise."* ~Sista Souljah

*"Just because your living does not mean you're alive."* ~ Kelis

*"Do not be afraid to stop at just a thought!"*
~Nina Elcock

*"Be a fox—Observe & trust your instincts when you sense danger."* ~Sherri Argov

*"Do something that feeds the soul."* ~Dr. Robin Smith

*"Don't be governed by wishful thinking."* ~Sherri Argov

*"If someone shows you who they are, believe them."* ~Unknown

*"Husbands can leave too! (Like the idea of being independent)"* ~Diva Diaries

*"It's so important to Do!"* ~Jada Pinkett Smith

*"We are never as critical of other people as we are of ourselves."* ~Nina Elcock

*"You can move with clarity if you know your purpose in life."* ~Pastor Waldrond

*"Never stop living your life! Take a class, develop a hobby, and meet people . . ."* ~Sherri Argov

*"Don't stop moving to your own rhythm."* ~Sherri Argrov

*"Hearts can have their own imagination."*
~Pastor AR Bernard

*"Change is deceitful, Beauty is vain but a woman who fears the Lord shall be praised."*
~Proverbs 31:30

*"Know what you deserve!"* ~Maria Mejias

*"Are recovering alcoholics really recovered if they cannot walk into a bar?"* ~Nina Elcock

*"Girls today need to make doubt their friend."*
~JadaPinkett Smith

*"We stay in relationships past their natural death."* ~Donna Marie Williams

*"You're going to mess up your future, if you can't get over the past."* ~Dr. Carolyn Showell

*"If I change my mindset, I can make better choices."* ~Dr. Carolyn Showell

*"The absence of someone should not change your desire."* ~Dr. Carolyn Showell

*"Mind your own business first."* ~Iyanla Vanzant

*Melissa Emily Mitchell*

# **A Poem for Nina**

*Nina is such a pretty name*
*It rings a tune like Nefertiti.*

*Anyway I met Nina—she is such a nice girl*
*We had a conversation about how nice she*
*was—too nice to the whole world.*

*The reason I wrote a poem for her is because we are*
*so much alike*
*You rarely cross paths with people whose similarities*
*are so perfect.*

*We both were hurt and are trying to overcome the*
*demands and hardships in this world.*

*She is not alone. I feel her pain.*

*Now we are two individuals with our heads together,*
*spitting knowledge and truth trying to survive the*
*struggles and the pain.*

*Girl, I reach out to you!*

# Letter to Ms. Giovanni

*Dear Ms. Giovanni:*

*The day I picked up your book "<u>Love Poems</u>" was the day you changed my life. You helped me get back into what I really love after taking a break—which is to express the way I feel through what I write.*

*When I began to write poetry, which was quite some time ago, I was afraid my writings were not good enough. Soon I would begin to know after understanding your writings and seeing how many of your poems have touched my life that one can express their emotions in simple ways because it is not about how many words you use as much as it is about what you say.*

*Thank you, Ms. Giovanni; I have begun the journey toward being a lifelong fan. I hope we can meet someday. Even exchange some words of faith and poetry. Thank you for your influence. I hope one day you become a lifelong fan of me.*

*Sincerely,*
*Melissa Emily Mitchell*

*Melissa Emily Mitchell*

*Dedicated to My Unborn*

# December (Formerly: The Gift I Lost in December)

*You were born into sadness and confusion*
*Things just weren't quite right*
*Mommy was unprepared and ignorant to raising*
*such a brand new life*
*I know you were a gift to me*
*Something beautiful and true*
*Now what's done is done*
*You're not here anymore and steadfastly I'm*
*missing you*
*You are a part of me—my golden child*
*I'll hold you close to heart*
*I'll never forget you*
*I promise I won't*
*Come here—let's start over—let's pretend . . .*
*let's start*
*Hey sweetie, how are you doing?*
*Mommy loves you! You know that*
*Mommy, you don't love me*
*Because if you felt the way you said*
*You would have never given me away already*
*dead*
*I wasn't even born—I was already dead*
*Baby I'm so sorry*

*It's just that sometimes in life you get caught up*
*No that's not it at all, the Lord interrupted: It is*
*that you ran out of man's worst creation called*
*Luck.*

# <u>Acknowledgements</u>

*One Faith, My Lord and Savior:*
<u>All </u>*things are possible through you! You are my source of strength. I am thirsty without you. Thank you for blessing me with this channel of expression called poetry. I truly believe that without this outlet and you, who is also the source of love and healing, I could not have made it through. I am so humbled by experience. I owe this all to you.*

*To Family and Friends:*
*For the constant encouragement, admiration, ideas, and faith in me, I am truly blessed and love you. To believe in self is one thing—but to see that others believe in you and your vision—means much much more . . .*

*One Muse, Ms. Nina Elcock:*
*You are an amazing friend and one of life's special treasures. We've come a long way from Antoinette's Café "with a verse, stanza or just a thought". Thank you for always opening your heart to me and your ears to my spoken words. You have always supported me and you know I will always support you! I love you girl fiercely!*

*Melissa Emily Mitchell*

*To My Favorite Poets:*
*Asha Bandele, Nikki Giovanni, Maya Angelou, Sonia Sanchez, Khalil Gibran, and Heru Ptah: I love each of you and although we haven't had the opportunity to meet, please know that you have influenced me with your poetry and your writings.*

*Tupac Amaru Shakur: You are an amazing poet who was taken from life too soon.*

*Special thanks to: Mommy, Daddy (May you R.I.P.), Pastor Michael Waldrond, Reverend Lakeisha Waldrond, Peter Hurley (Photographer), Danielle Thomas (Dear Friend and Stylist), Francisco (Make-up Artist), Ivonne Ramirez, Veronica Colon, Maria Mejias, and many more . . .*

# About the Author

*Melissa Emily Mitchell was born and raised in New York City. She is a passionate writer who has been writing contemporary poetry since 1997. Her first poems were inspired by her journal entries and random thoughts. Over time, the subject matter of her poetry intensified as her experiences with love and life deepened.*

*Melissa enjoys reading and writing poetry, performing spoken word and developing other projects connected to her passion for verse. "Come Into My Place: A Collection of Love Poems" is*

*Melissa's first collection of work. She is currently working on her future projects which include a 2012 calendar, poetry on wall art, and another collection of poems.*